Filet Crochet

Filet Crochet

Pam Dawson

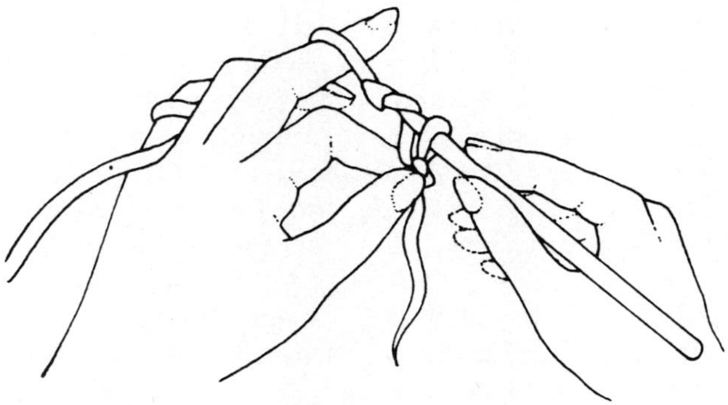

SEARCH PRESS

Introduction

Unlike many other crafts, the initial expense when experimenting with crochet is minimal. You only need a crochet hook and a few balls of yarn to explore the possibilities of various techniques and extend your knowledge of the craft.

As well as being economical in price and practical in application, all crochet is simple in execution. It is compact and portable and, unlike knitting, you do not run the risk of stitches slipping off the needles, so it can easily be carried wherever you go. It is an extremely fast way of achieving exciting results, without enduring tedious weeks of endeavour and, with the exception of Tunisian crochet, there is only one working loop on the hook as each stitch is completed, so crochet can be picked up and put down with ease, without running the risk of making a mistake in a pattern.

All forms of crochet are versatile but my own favourite technique is filet crochet, which can be adapted in so many different ways. The French word for 'net' is 'filet' and this accurately describes the openwork background which forms the basis of filet crochet. This basic net background provides a lacy fabric in its own right and has a variety of uses. Into this background, geometric shapes, or intricate motifs can be incorporated by using solid blocks of trebles and simple variations, to create exciting pictorial effects. Once the background net has been completed, a woven effect can be achieved by threading separate contrasting yarns through the holes in the net, or a tufted fabric created by knotting short lengths of yarn into the net background, similar to the method used for rug making.

As filet crochet uses only three basic stitches—chains, double crochet and trebles—it is easy to master this attractive technique, and even a beginner will be able to follow the step-by-step basic instructions and illustrations of the methods given in this book. More experienced crochet devotees will be delighted to discover the scope this technique has to offer and will be encouraged to experiment with their own designs.

Opposite: ***this simple cot or pram cover would make an ideal gift for the new arrival.*** ***See page 24 for instructions***

Tools and materials

Apart from a crochet hook and suitable yarn, as you progress to making garments, the following items are essential. You will probably find they are already available and just need gathering together before you begin your first project:-

A small, sharp pair of scissors
A rigid rule for measuring tension
A tape measure for checking garment sections
A blunt-ended sewing needle
A clean, white cloth for pressing, when required

Crochet hooks

Crochet only requires a single hook and for most techniques, the exception being Tunisian crochet, these are produced in a short, easily-manageable length, with a hook at one end. For those who may experience difficulty in holding a short hook, some sizes can be obtained complete with a handle.

Modern hooks are available in a range of metric sizes and this metric figure is based on the exact diameter of the shank of the hook in millimetres. The larger the metric figure, the greater the diameter of the hook. The smallest sizes are manufactured in steel for rigidity and the largest sizes are made from lightweight alloys, so that they are not too heavy to handle.

Suitable yarns

The generic term for any spun fibre, whatever its structure or composition, is 'yarn'. This covers everything from pure wool, cotton or silk to man-made fibres such as nylon or acrylic, and includes any combination of these qualities in varying proportions.

These qualities are blended together, spun, twisted and crimped to give an enormous range of yarns but an old maxim should apply when beginning to experiment with different fabrics—'pick the right yarn for the right job'. When working filet crochet, the clean, crisp outlines of a pattern will probably look best if they are worked in a smooth yarn such as cotton. Some motifs lend themselves to a softer, more romantic look, and for these, a fine mohair is the ideal choice.

If you are a complete novice, however, use a smooth double knitting quality until you become familiar with the basic steps and can manipulate the hook and yarn with ease.

Abbreviations and tension

Before beginning to work from a published pattern, two requirements are essential: a knowledge of the terminology used in an abbreviated form and the important part correct tension plays in the structure of the fabric.

Abbreviations used in this book

alt	alternate(ly)
beg	begin(ning)
blk(s)	block(s)
ch	chain(s)
cm	centimetre(s)
cont	continu(e))(ing)
dc	double crochet (USA single crochet)
dec	decreas(e) (ing)
DK	double knitting
foll	following
g	gramme(s)
htr	half treble (USA half double crochet)
in	inch(es)

K	knit
mm	millimetre
P	purl
patt	pattern
rem	remain(ing)
rep	repeat(ing
Rs	right side of fabric
ss	slip stitch(es)
sp(s)	space(s)
st(s)	stitch(es)
tog	together
tr	treble(s) (USA double crochet)
Ws	wrong side of fabric
yrh	yarn round hook

Tension

The simplest way to explain the importance of tension is to use a dressmaking pattern as an example. This will tell you how many metres you require of various types of fabrics but it doesn't matter if the pattern needs taffeta or tweed, as one metre in width and length will be exactly the same.

In crochet, however, you are combining the skills of a weaver and a dressmaker to produce a fabric, and the type of yarn and hook size used will determine the number of stitches and rows needed to arrive at a given measurement.

Once you have mastered the basic steps, you will be working in a way which is comfortable for you, and this will also affect your tension. There is no such thing as an 'average' tension and you may work a little too loosely, or too tightly to achieve the correct tension given in the pattern, which will have been achieved by the original designer and upon which all the eventual calculations for the design will have been based. When beginning any pattern, therefore, work a tension sample to make sure you can achieve the correct number of stitches and rows to the given measurement, or your garment will end up much too small or too large.

How to check your tension

Work a sample, using the hook, yarn and stitch given in the pattern and measure this sample to make sure it is to the size given under the heading, 'Tension', in the pattern, (see Fig. 1).

If your sample measures *less* than the size given, you are working too tightly and you should change to one, or more, sizes larger hook to overcome this. If your sample measures *more* than the size given, you are working too loosely and you should change to one, or more, sizes smaller hook to overcome this.

If you can achieve the correct tension in width but not the correct tension in depth, it is fairly safe to begin the pattern, as length can usually be adjusted by working more or fewer rows to arrive at the correct measurement.

It doesn't matter how many times you have to change hook sizes up or down, but unless you take the time to check this vital step, you cannot guarantee satisfactory results.

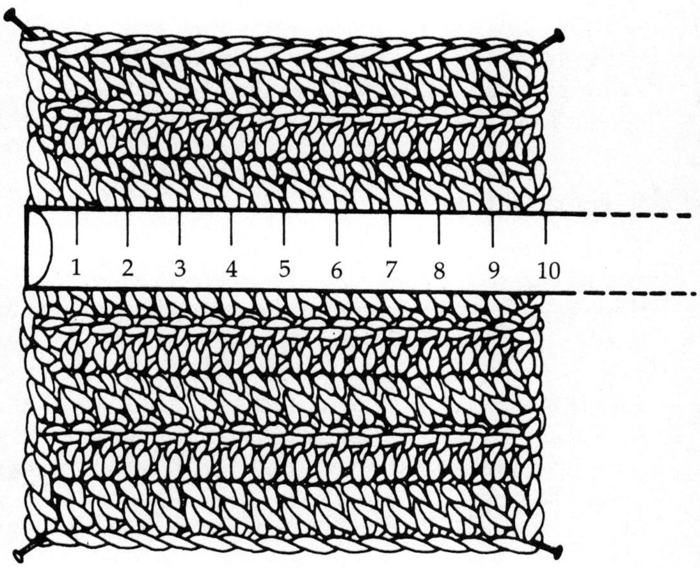

fig 1 how to check your tension

Helping hand

If you are a newcomer to crochet, the following information will be of help to you.

Slip loop

All crochet begins with a slip loop on the hook. It is a working loop only and does not count as a stitch.
To make a slip loop, take the main end from a ball of yarn across the short end and use the curve of the hook to draw the main length through from the back to the front. Tighten this loop and leave it on the crochet hook, (see Fig. 2).

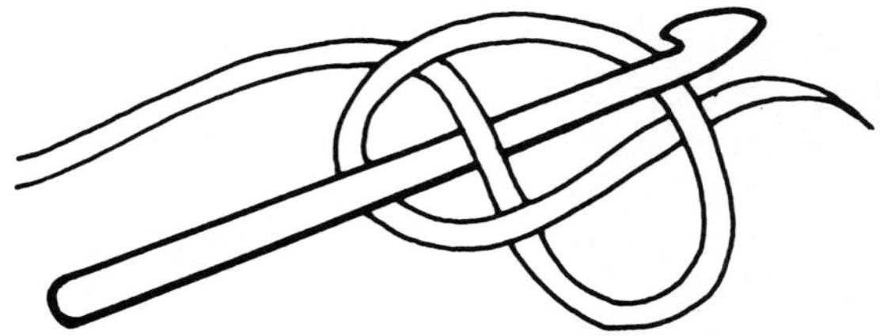

fig 2 ***making a slip loop***

Chain stitches

With the hook in your right hand and the yarn in your left hand, make a series of chain stitches to form the foundation row.
*Catch the yarn in the curve of the hook and draw the yarn through the slip loop on the hook from the back to the front. This makes one chain and the working loop remains on the hook, (see Fig. 3).
Repeat from the * for the required number of chains.

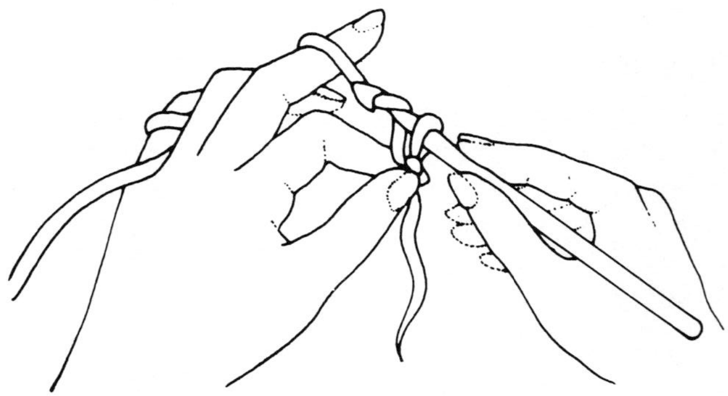

fig 3 ***making a chain***

Slip stitches

These shallow stitches are used as a means of shaping and to get from one place to another in a row.
*Insert the hook from the front to the back under one loop of a commencing chain, or both loops at the top of the stitch where the slip loop is required, catch the yarn in the curve of the hook and draw a loop through, then through the slip loop on the hook. This makes one slip stitch and the working loop remains on the hook, (see Fig. 4).
Repeat from the * for the required number of slip stitches.

fig 4 ***making slip stitches***

Double crochet stitches

Make the required number of chains, plus one extra turning chain, which is needed to bring the hook up to the correct height to work the stitches. 21 chains will make 20 double crochet stitches.

Miss the first 2 chains, *insert the hook through the top loop of the next chain, catch the yarn in the curve of the hook and draw a loop through the chain, then catch the yarn in the hook again and draw through both loops on hook. The 2 missed chains count as the first stitch, one double crochet has been made and the working loop remains on the hook, (see Fig. 5).

Repeat from the * for the required number of double crochet stitches.

On subsequent rows, begin with 2 chains to count as the first stitch, work 1 double crochet under the 2 loops at the top of the 2nd stitch and every following stitch to the end of the row, (see Fig. 6).

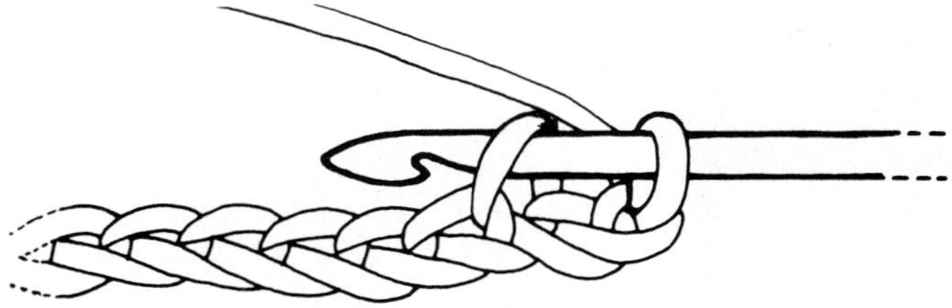

fig 5 ***working double crochet stitches into a chain***

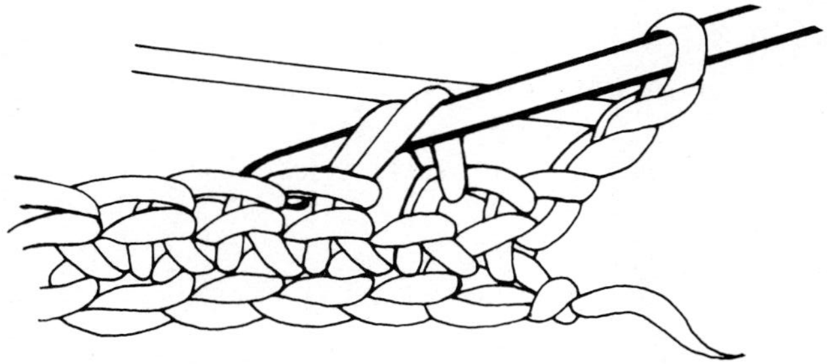

fig 6 ***working subsequent rows of double crochet***

Half treble stitches

Make the required number of chains as for double crochet stitches.

Miss the first 2 chains, *put the yarn round the hook, insert the hook through the top loop of the next chain, catch the yarn in the curve of the hook and draw a loop through the chain, catch the yarn in the curve of the hook again and draw through all 3 loops on hook. The 2 missed chains count as the first stitch, one half treble has been worked and the working loop remains on the hook, (see Fig. 7).

Repeat from the * for the required number of half treble stitches.

On subsequent rows, begin with 2 chains to count as the first stitch, work 1 half treble under the 2 loops at the top of the 2nd stitch and every following stitch to the end of the row, (see Fig. 8).

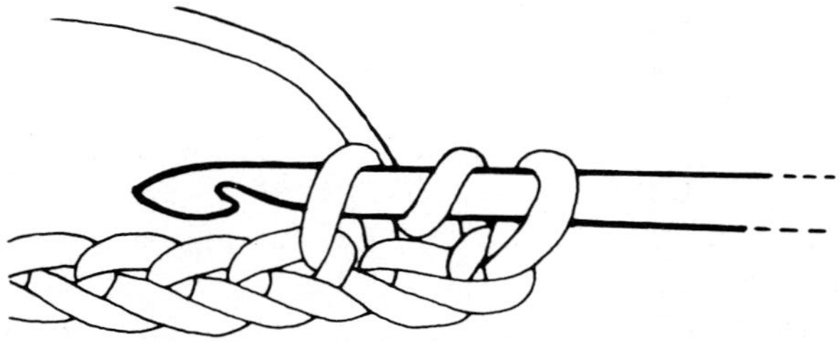

fig 7 ***working half treble stitches into a chain***

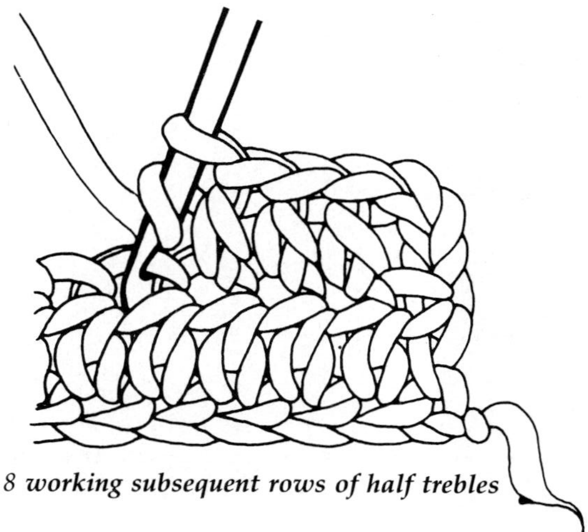

fig 8 ***working subsequent rows of half trebles***

Treble stitches

Make the required number of chains, plus two extra turning chains, to bring the hook up to the correct height to work the stitches. 22 chains will make 20 treble stitches.

Miss the first 3 chains, *put the yarn round the hook, insert the hook through the top loop of the next chain, catch the yarn in the curve of the hook and draw a loop through the chain, (catch the yarn in the curve of the hook and draw through 2 loops on the hook) twice. The 3 missed chains count as the first stitch, one treble has been made and the working loop remains on the hook, (see Fig. 9).

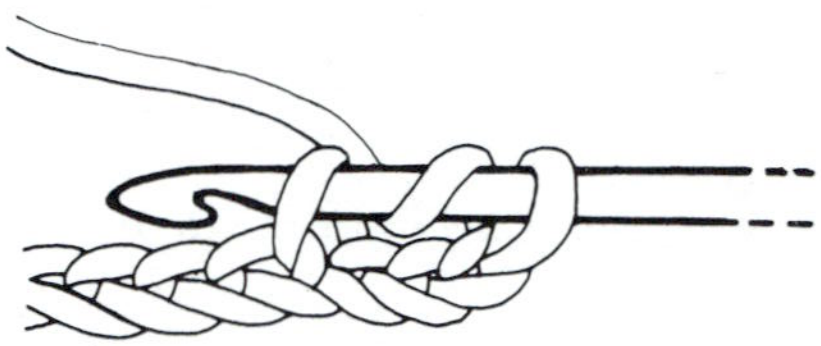

fig 9 ***working treble stitches into a chain***

Repeat from the * for the required number of treble stitches.

On subsequent rows, begin with 3 chains to count as the first stitch, work 1 treble under the 2 loops at the top of the 2nd stitch and every following stitch to the end of the row, (see Fig. 10).

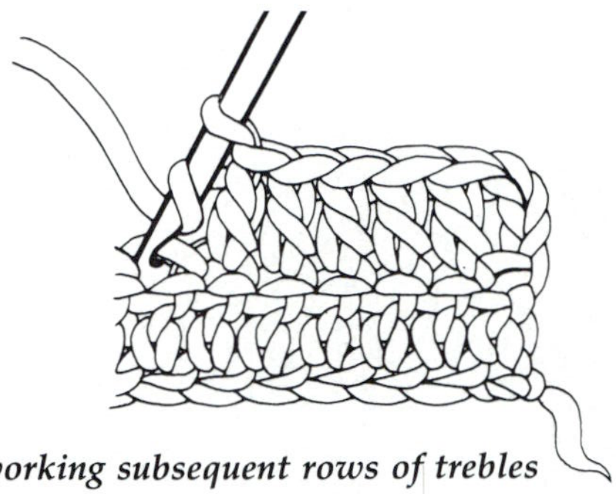

fig 10 ***working subsequent rows of trebles***

This crisp, white cafe curtain would grace any window, see page 41 for instructions.

How to begin

Traditional filet crochet methods produce a flat fabric where areas of solid patterns are joined together by an openwork background. The stitch groups which form the fabric are as follows:

Spaces: the net background.

Blocks: the solid shapes on the net background, formed by working groups of trebles.

Lacets: small 'v' shapes, formed by working a double crochet in a block, instead of a treble.

Bars: linking chains worked over a lacet, or bar, in the previous row.

These patterns are normally worked in rows, by turning the work at the end of each row, ready to begin the next row. The instructions are given in chart form, where each stitch group is represented by a different symbol.

How to work spaces

Unless otherwise stated in the design instructions, each space is made up of two chains plus a linking treble and is normally shown on a filet crochet chart as an open square.

When working spaces from a chart, allow two chains and one treble for every open square, plus one extra treble which is worked as three chains to begin the row, or a treble to end the row.

To begin the first row, miss the first seven chains, allowing two of these to form the space along the lower edge, three to form the first treble of the row and the last two to form the space on the row being worked, work one treble into the eighth chain from the hook to complete the first space, (see Fig. 11).

How to work blocks

Unless otherwise stated in the design instructions, each block is made up of three trebles and is normally shown on a filet crochet chart as a solid square.

fig 11 ***how to work spaces***

fig 12 ***how to work blocks***

When working blocks from a chart, allow three trebles for each solid square, plus one extra treble which is worked as three chains to begin the row, or a treble to end the row. A single block needs four trebles; two blocks seven trebles; three blocks ten trebles, and so on.

To begin the first row, miss the first three chains to count as the first treble, work the second treble of the block into the fourth chain from the hook, the third treble of the block into the fifth chain from the hook, then work one treble into the next chain to complete the first block, (see Fig. 12).

How to work lacets

Unless otherwise stated in the design instructions, each lacet is made up of three chains, a double crochet, three chains and a linking treble. It is normally shown as a 'v' over *two* squares on a filet crochet chart.

When working lacets from a chart, make three chains, miss two chains of a space, or two trebles of a block in the previous row, work a double crochet into the next treble, make three chains, miss two chains of a space or two trebles of a block in the previous row and work one treble into the next linking treble. This completes one lacet, (see Fig. 13).

Lacets should not be worked at the beginning or end of a row, as they tend to pull the side edges out of shape.

fig 13 ***how to work lacets***

How to work bars

Unless otherwise stated in the design instructions, each bar is made up of five chains plus a linking treble. It is normally shown as a dash, -, over *two* squares on a filet crochet chart.

When working bars from a chart, make five chains, miss one complete lacet, or bar, in the previous row and work one treble into the next linking treble. This completes one bar, (see Fig. 14).

Bars should not be worked at the beginning or end of a row, as they tend to pull the sides edges out of shape. Their main purpose is to bring the row being worked up to the correct level, after working a lacet in the previous row. They can also be worked over a bar in the previous row, to form a double space in the fabric.

fig 14 ***how to work bars***

Shaping in filet crochet

Decreasing or increasing in filet crochet can be worked in two ways. The first method decreases or increases a complete space, or block, and can only be worked at the beginning or end of a row. This shaping forms a series of 'steps' at the side edges.

The second method decreases or increases just one chain of a space, or one treble of a block, either at the edges or where required in a row, and this is repeated until a complete space, or block, has been decreased or increased. This method forms a gradual slope and is the ideal way of shaping a garment at the underarm, or neck edge.

Decreasing in spaces

To decrease a complete space at the beginning of a row, slip stitch across the first 3 stitches of the space in the previous row, then into the 4th stitch. Make 5 chains to count as the first treble and 2 chains of the next space, work 1 treble into the next treble and pattern to the end of the row, (see Fig. 15).

To decrease a complete space at the end of a row, pattern to the last space of the previous row, leave this space unworked, turn the work, ready to pattern the next row, (see Fig. 16).

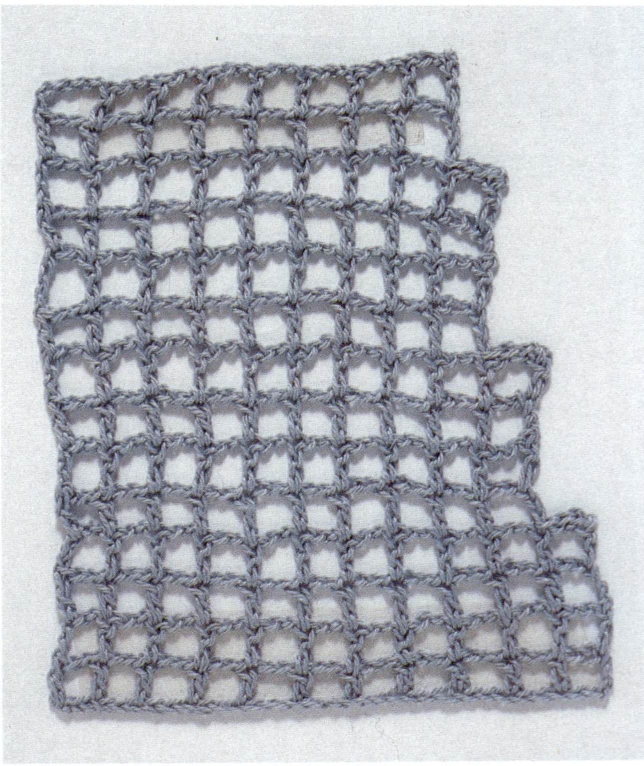

fig 15 ***decreasing a complete space at the beginning of a row***

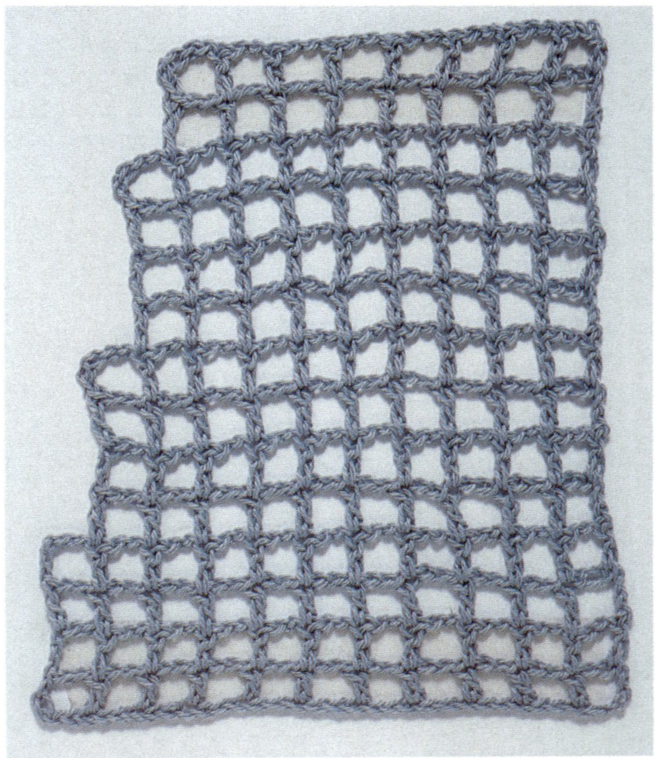

fig 16 ***decreasing a complete space at the end of a row***

To decrease a single stitch at the beginning of every alternate row, work as follows:

1) For the first step of the decrease, make 4 chains instead of 5, then pattern to the end of the row.

2) On the next row, work to the last space, 1 chain, miss 1 chain, 1 treble into the 3rd of the first 4 chains.

3) For the second step of the decrease, make 3 chains to count as the first treble, miss 1 chain, pattern to the end of the row.

4) On the next row, work to the last treble and 3 chains, miss the treble and work 1 treble into the 3rd of the first 3 chains.

One complete space has been decreased. Either repeat these 4 steps until the required number of spaces have been decreased, (see Fig. 17), or continue working in pattern in the usual way.

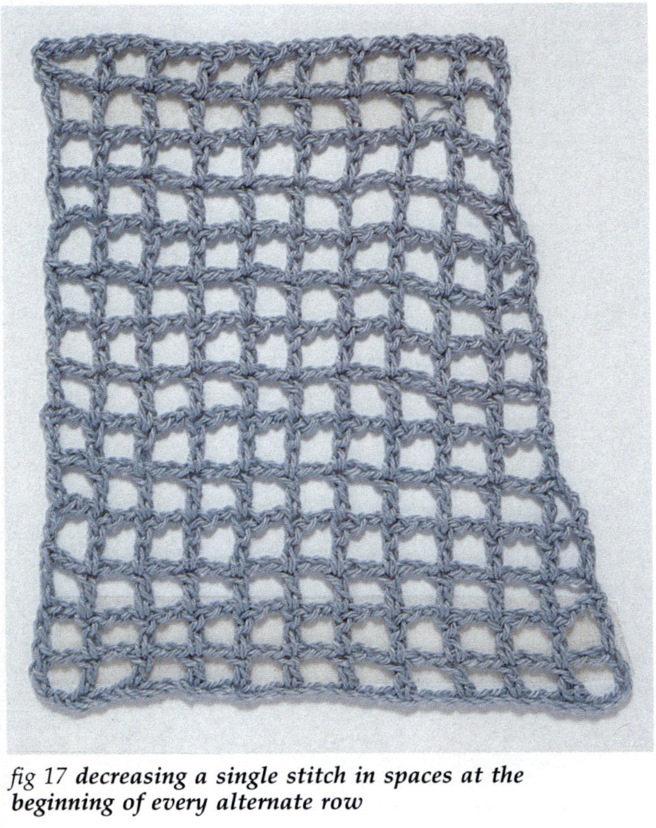

fig 17 ***decreasing a single stitch in spaces at the beginning of every alternate row***

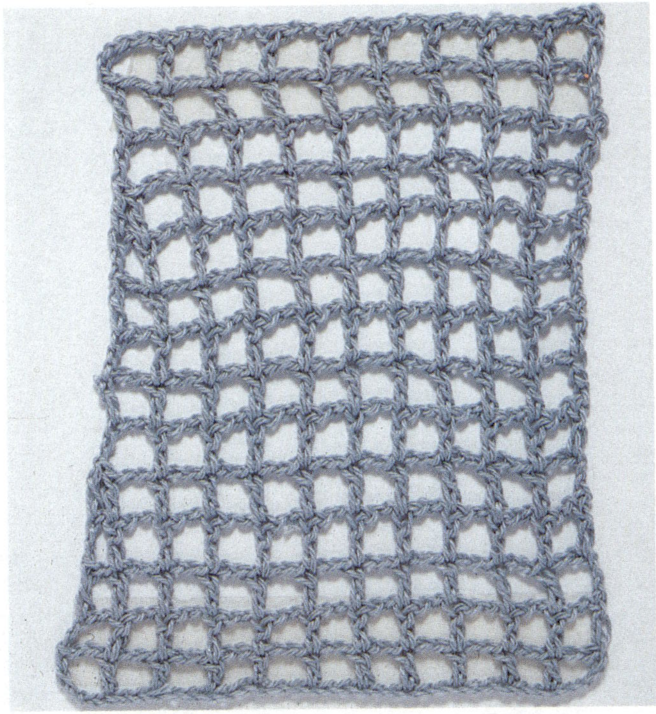

fig 18 ***decreasing a single stitch in spaces at the end of every alternate row***

To decrease a single stitch at the end of every alternate row, work as follows:

1) For the first step of the decrease, pattern to the last space, 1 chain, miss 2 chains, 1 treble into the 3rd of the 5 chains at the beginning of the previous row.

2) On the next row, make 4 chains to count as the first treble and 1 chain space, 1 treble into treble, pattern to the end of the row.

3) For the second step of the decrease, pattern to the last space, miss 1 chain, 1 treble into the 3rd of the 4 chains at the beginning of the previous row.

4) On the next row, make 5 chains to count as the first treble and 2 chain space, miss first 2 trebles, 1 treble into next treble, pattern to the end of the row.

One complete space has been decreased. Either repeat these 4 steps until the required number of spaces have been decreased, (see Fig. 18), or continue working in pattern in the usual way.

Decreasing in blocks

To decrease a complete block at the beginning of a row, slip stitch across the first 3 stitches of the block in the previous row, then into the 4th stitch. Make 3 chains to count as the first treble and pattern to the end of the row, (see Fig. 19).

fig 19 ***decreasing a complete block at the beginning of a row***

To decrease a complete block at the end of a row, pattern to the last block of the previous row, leave this block unworked, turn the work, ready to pattern the next row, (see Fig. 20).

fig 20 ***decreasing a complete block at the end of a row***

To decrease a single stitch at the beginning of every alternate row, work as follows:

1) For the first step of the decrease, make 3 chains to count as the first treble, miss first treble, work next 2 trebles together, 1 treble into next treble to complete the block, pattern to the end of the row.

2) On the next row, pattern to the last 2 trebles, 1 treble into the next treble, 1 treble into the 3rd of the first 3 chains.

Repeat stages 1 and 2 twice more. One complete block has been decreased. Either repeat these steps until the required number of blocks have been decreased, (see Fig. 21), or continue working in pattern in the usual way.

fig 21 ***decreasing a single stitch in blocks at the beginning of every alternate row***

To decrease a single stitch at the end of every alternate row, work as follows:

1) For the first step of the decrease, pattern to the last 3 trebles, work the next 2 trebles together, 1 treble into the 3rd of the first 3 chains at the beginning of the previous row.

2) On the next row, work 3 chains to count as the first treble, 1 treble into the next treble, 1 treble into the next treble to complete the block, pattern to the end of the row.

Repeat stages 1 and 2 twice more. One complete block has been decreased. Either repeat these steps until the required number of blocks have been decreased, (see Fig. 22), or continue working in pattern in the usual way.

fig 22 ***decreasing a single stitch in blocks at the end of every alternate row***

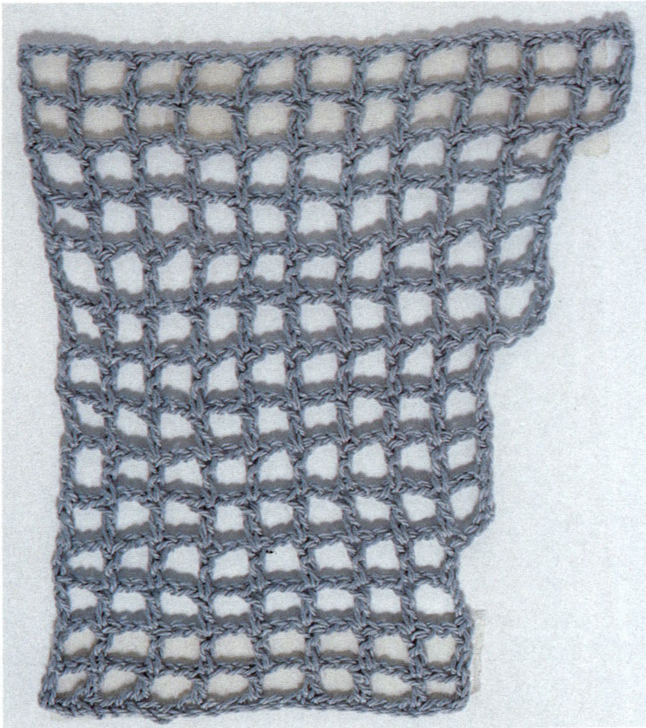

fig 23 ***increasing a complete space at the beginning of a row***

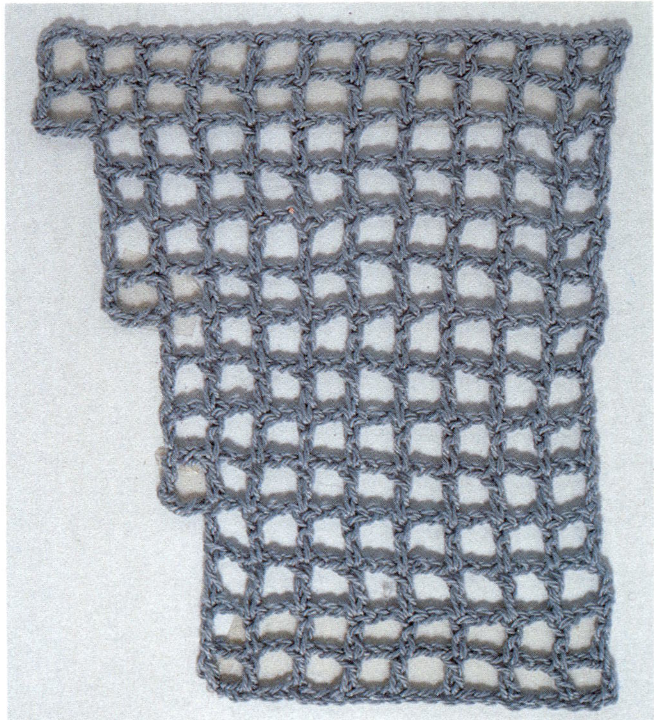

fig 24 ***increasing a complete space at the end of a row***

Increasing in spaces

To increase a complete space at the beginning of a row, make 7 extra chains; 2 to count as the lower edge of the space, 3 as the first treble and 2 as the top edge of the space. Work 1 treble into the top of the last stitch of the previous row to complete the space, then pattern to the end of the row, (see Fig. 23).

To increase a complete space at the end of a row, pattern to the end of the row then work 1 quadruple treble, (yarn round hook 4 times to begin the stitch), into the base of the last treble of the row, (see Fig. 24).

To increase a single stitch at the beginning of every alternate row, work as follows:

1) For the first step of the increase, make 6 chains instead of 5, then pattern to the end of the row.

2) On the next row, work to the last space, 2 chains, miss 2 chains, 1 treble into next chain, 1 treble into the 3rd of the first 6 chains of previous row.

3) For the second step of the increase, make 4 chains to count as the first treble and 1 chain space, miss first treble, 1 treble into next treble, pattern to the end of the row.

4) On the next row, work to the last space, 1 chain, miss 1 chain, 1 treble into the 3rd of the first 4 chains of the previous row. Work the next 2 rows in the usual way.

One complete space has been increased. Either repeat these 4 steps until the required number of spaces have been increased, (see Fig. 25), or continue working in pattern in the usual way.

To increase a single stitch at the end of every alternate row, work as follows:

1) For the first step of the increase, work to the last space, make 3 chains instead of 2, 1 treble into 3rd of first 5 chains of previous row.

2) On the next row, make 3 chains to count as first treble, miss first treble, 1 treble into next chain, pattern to the end of the row.

3) For the second step of the increase, pattern to the last 2 trebles, 1 treble into the next treble, 1 chain, 1 treble into the 3rd of first 3 chains of previous row.

4) On the next row, make 4 chains to count as first treble and 1 chain space, 1 treble into next treble, pattern to the end of the row. Work the next 2 rows in the usual way, ending next row with 1 treble into 3rd of first 4 chains of previous row.

One complete space has been increased. Either repeat these 4 steps until the required number of spaces have been increased, (see Fig. 26), or continue working in pattern in the usual way.

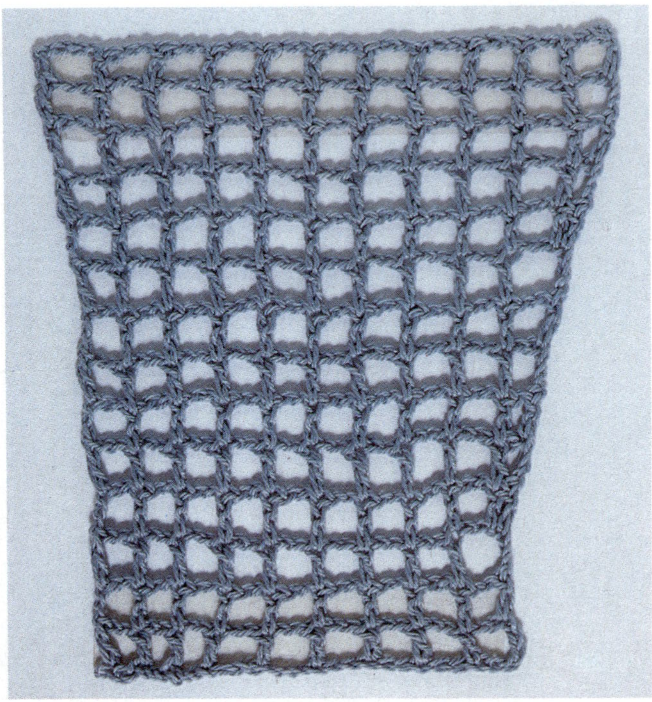

fig 25 ***increasing a single stitch in spaces at the beginning of every alternate row***

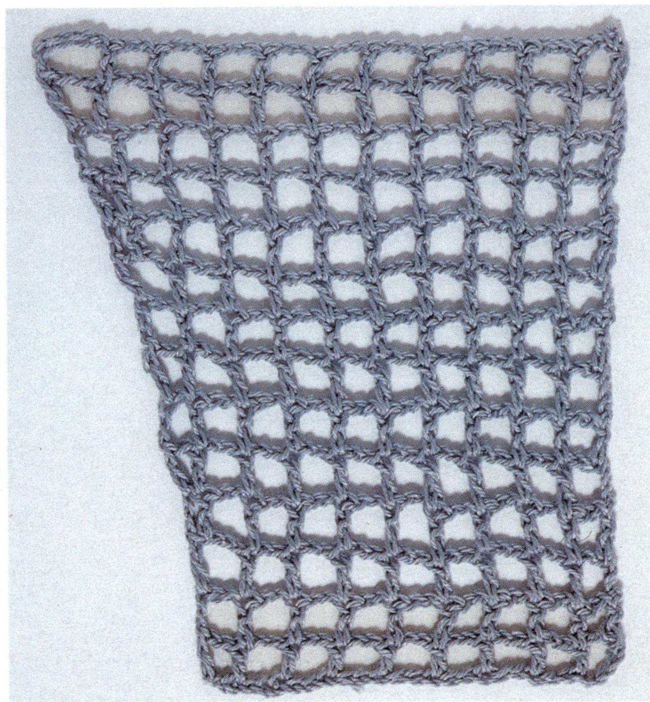

fig 26 ***increasing a single stitch in spaces at the end of every alternate row***

Increasing in blocks

To increase a complete block at the beginning of a row, make 5 extra chains, 2 to count as the lower edge of the block and 3 as the first treble. Work 1 treble into the 4th chain from the hook, 1 treble into next chain and 1 treble into the last stitch of the previous row, then pattern to the end of the row, (see Fig. 27).

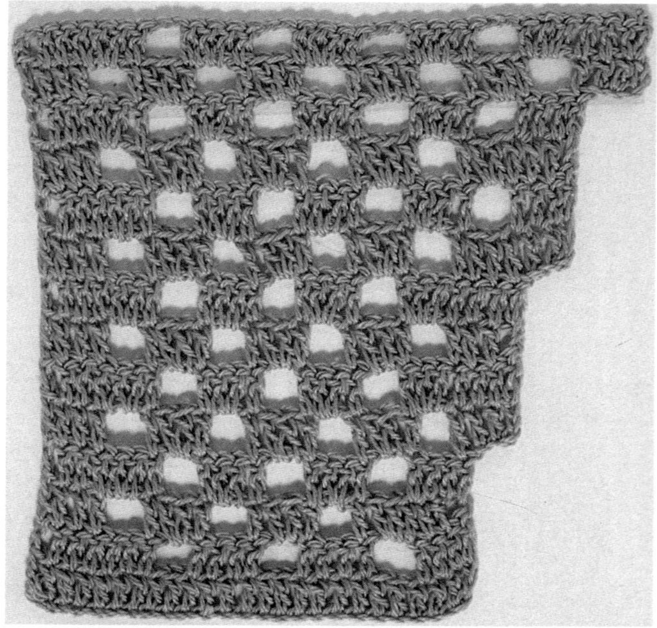

fig 27 ***increasing a complete block at the beginning of a row***

To increase a complete block at the end of a row, pattern to the end of the row then work 1 double treble, (yarn round hook twice to begin the stitch), into the base of the last treble, (1 double treble into base of last double treble) twice, (see Fig. 28).

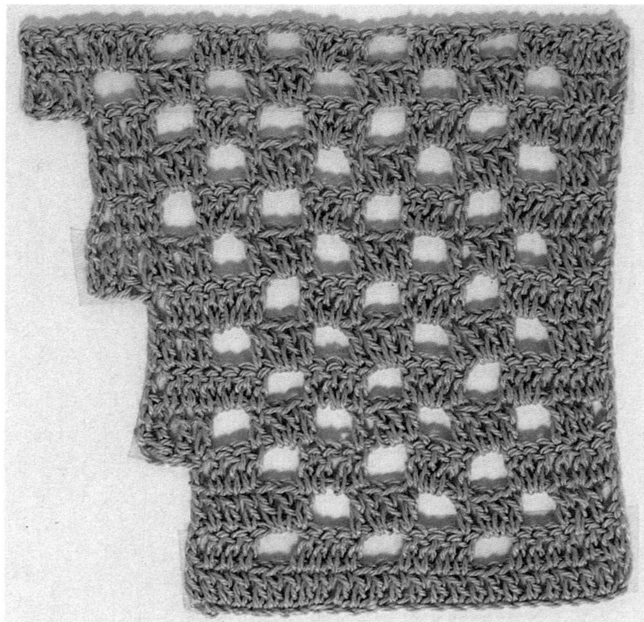

fig 28 ***increasing a complete block at the end of a row***

To increase a single stitch at the beginning of every alternate row, work as follows:

1) For the first step of the increase, make 3 chains to count as the first treble and work 1 treble into the top of the first treble of the previous row instead of missing it, pattern to the end of the row.

2) On the next row, pattern to the last 2 trebles, 1 treble into the next treble, 1 treble into the 3rd of the first 3 chains.

Repeat steps 1 and 2 until one complete block has been increased, then either continue repeating the steps until the required number of blocks have been increased, (see Fig. 29), or work in pattern in the usual way.

fig 29 ***increasing a single stitch in blocks at the beginning of every alternate row***

To increase a single stitch at the end of every alternate row, work as follows:

1) For the first step of the increase, work to the last 2 trebles, work 2 trebles into the top of the next treble instead of 1, 1 treble into the 3rd of the first 3 chains.

2) On the next row, work 3 chains to count as the first treble, miss first treble, 1 treble into next treble, pattern to the end of the row.

Repeat steps 1 and 2 until one complete block has been increased, then either continue repeating the steps until the required number of blocks have been increased, (see Fig. 30), or work in pattern in the usual way.

fig 30 ***increasing a single stitch in blocks at the end of every alternate row***

Woven and looped fabrics

On to a background of filet spaces, separate strands of yarn can be woven or looped to produce unusual and exciting fabrics. The woven effect is particularly attractive for cot blankets or rugs and the looped effect makes a marvellous mock fur fabric, suitable for collars and cuffs on a jacket. Worked in thick cotton, the looped method can be used for bath or kitchen mats.

Woven fabric

Make the required area of filet net background but using only one chain for each space and working half trebles instead of trebles for each linking stitch. To achieve this, make a number of commencing chains which can be divided by 2 plus 1, eg 21 chains. Work the first half treble into the 5th chain from the hook on the 1st row and begin subsequent rows with 3 chains.

Cut lengths of contrast coloured yarns to the same length as the net background, allowing an additional 4–10cm (1½–4in) to be taken up in weaving. These ends can be turned under and secured or left free to form a fringed effect.

With the right side of the background facing you, thread 2 or more strands of yarn into a blunt-ended sewing needle. Begin at the lower right-hand edge of the net and thread the yarn under the first chain space in the first row and over the first chain space in the 2nd row, then continue in this way to the top right-hand edge.

Begin again at the lower right-hand edge, taking the yarn over the 2nd chain space in the first row and under the 2nd chain space in the 2nd row to alternate the position of the weaving, then continue in this way to the top right-hand edge.

Continue in this way until the entire background has been covered, varying the colours as required, (see Fig. 31).

fig 31 ***sample of woven fabric***

Looped fabric

Make the filet net background as given for the woven fabric.

To work the loops, cut yarn into lengths of approximately 10–12cm (4–5in), take 2 or more strands and fold these in half.

With the right side of the background facing you, work in a horizontal direction along the rows. Insert a crochet hook from the front under the first 1 chain space of the 1st row and out to the front again, place the folded loops of yarn over the hook and pull these through the space. Place the cut ends of yarn over the hook again and draw these through the loops on the hook, pulling them up tightly to secure the knot.

Repeat this action into every chain space, or alternate chain space on every row, or every alternate row, depending on the thickness of fabric required, (see Fig. 32).

fig 32 ***sample of looped fabric***

Baby's pram cover

This design is simple enough for the complete beginner to start experimenting with crochet. It is quick to work and can be made to any size, or in any suitable baby yarn. It is also a wonderful way of trying out colour combinations and using up oddments of yarn.

Size

18in/46cm wide by 24in/61cm long, allowing for 3in/7.5cm turned down at top; width and length are adjustable but note that quantities given will differ

You will need

3 × 40g balls of Baby DK weight in main colour A
1 ball of same in each of 4 contrast colours, or oddments of DK
3.50mm crochet hook
The yarn quantities are based on average requirements and are therefore approximate

Tension

25sts and 11 rows of sps to 4in/10cm over filet crochet background worked on 3.50mm hook

Background

With 3.50mm hook and A, make 110ch and beg at lower edge. To increase or decrease width, add or subtract 6ch for each 1in/2.5cm required.
1st row (Rs) 1tr into 8th ch from hook, *2ch, miss 2ch, ltr in next ch, rep from * to end. 106 sts—35 sps.
2nd row 5ch as first tr and 2ch, 1tr in next tr, *2ch, 1tr in next tr, rep from * to end, working last tr in 3rd of first 7ch. OR 35 sps.
3rd row 5ch as first tr and 2ch, 1tr in next tr, *2ch, 1tr in next tr, rep from * to end, working last tr in 3rd of first 5ch.
Rep last row until background measures 24in/61cm from beg, or required length allowing 3in/7.5cm for turned down top edge.
Fasten off.

Weaving

Take the end from the centre and the end from the outside of a ball of contrast yarn and thread these 2 ends into a blunt-ended sewing needle, or cut 2 lengths from oddments of yarn approximately 56in/142cm long.
With the Rs of the background facing, leave about 4in/10cm ends for the fringing, beg at the top edge and weave the yarn under and over into each sp to the lower edge, making sure the yarn is not pulled through too tightly.
Turn and work back into the same sps again but reverse the position of the under and over threads. Cut the yarn, leaving 4in/10cm ends for the fringing.
Alternating the colours as required, work into each row of the background in this way.

Edging for sides and bottom

Trim the fringing to the required length, again checking that the yarn has not been pulled through too tightly and that the background is to the correct length.
Fold down 3in/7.5cm at the top edge to the Rs. With the Rs of work facing, 3.50mm hook and A, work through double and single thicknesses along side edge as foll:
Join with a ss to ch sp at side edge of cover, work 1ch to count as first dc, (1htr, 1tr, 1htr, 1dc) all into same sp, *miss 1 sp, work (1dc, 1htr, 1tr, 1htr, 1dc) into each sp down side edge, then along sps at lower edge and up other side edge.
Fasten off.

Edging for top

With 3.50mm hook and A make 90ch, or sufficient to go across top edge of cover, adding or substracting 8ch for each 1in/2.5cm required.

Next row Into 3rd ch from hook work 1htr, 1tr, 1htr, 1dc, *miss 3ch, work (1dc, 1htr, 1tr, 1htr, 1dc) into next ch, rep from * to end. Fasten off.

To complete

Press according to instuctions on ball band.

Darn in all ends.

Sew top edging along top edge of cover, securing the fringing.

Beach wrap

This long-line, wrap-over jacket makes an ideal beach wrap but would look just as effective worked in a plain double-knitting yarn and teamed with trousers.

Size

To fit 34–38in/86–97cm bust loosely
Actual measurement 46in/58.5cm
Length 32in/81cm
Sleeve seam 9in/23cm

You will need

15 × 50g balls of fancy yarn (DK weight)
3.50mm and 4.00mm crochet hooks
The yarn quantities are based on average requirements and are therefore approximate

Tension

21 sts and 9 rows to 4in/10cm over patt worked on 4.00mm hook

Back

With 4.00mm hook make 126ch.

1st row (Rs) 1tr in 4th ch from hook, 1tr in each of next 5ch, *(2ch, miss 2ch, 1tr in next ch) twice, 1tr in each of next 3ch, (2ch, miss 2ch, 1tr in next ch) twice, 1tr in each of next 9ch, rep from * to last 21ch, (2ch, miss 2ch, 1tr in next ch) twice, 1tr in each of next 3ch, (2ch, miss 2ch, 1tr in next ch) twice, 1tr in each of next 6ch. 124 sts, (41 blks or sps). This row reads as 2 blks, (2 sps, 1 blk, 2 sps, 3 blks) to last 21 sts, 2 sps, 1 blk, 2 sps, 2 blks.

2nd row 3ch as first tr, 1tr in each of next 3tr, *2ch, miss 2tr, 1tr in next tr, 2ch, 1tr in next tr, 2tr in sp, 1tr in next tr, 2ch, miss 2tr, 1tr in next tr, 2tr in sp, 1tr in next tr, 2ch, 1tr in next tr, 2ch, miss 2tr, 1tr in each of next 4tr, rep from * to end, working last tr into turning ch, (OR 1 blk, (2 sps, 1 blk, 1 sp, 1 blk, 2 sps, 1 blk) to end).

3rd row 5ch as first tr and 2ch, miss 2tr, 1tr in next tr, *2ch, 1tr in next tr, 2tr in sp, 1tr in next tr, 2ch, miss 2tr, 1tr in next tr, 2ch, 1tr in next tr, 2ch, miss 2tr, 1tr in next tr, 2tr in sp, 1tr in next tr, 2ch, 1tr in next tr, 2ch, miss 2tr, 1tr in next tr, rep from * to end, working last tr into turning ch, (OR 2 sps, (1 blk, 3 sps) to last 9 sts, 1 blk, 2 sps).

4th row 1 sp, *(1 blk, 2 sps) twice, 1 blk, 1 sp, rep from * to end.

5th row 1 blk, (2 sps, 3 blks, 2 sps, 1 blk) to end.

Cont in patt from chart until 76 rows in all have been worked. Fasten off.

chart for beach wrap

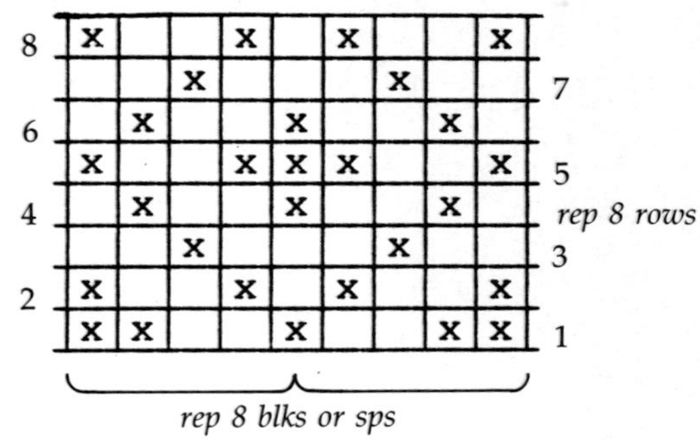

Opposite: ***we have used a slub yarn for this loosely-fitting jacket, which has a dropped shoulder-line. The sleeves are elbow length but you can make them to any length – remember to allow extra yarn!***

Left front

With 4.00mm hook make 102ch and work 36 rows in patt as on back. 100 sts, (33 blks or sps). **

Shape front edge

Next row Patt to last blk, turn and patt to end.
Keeping patt correct, dec one blk or sp at front edge on every alt row until 40 sts rem, (13 blks or sps), ending with a Ws row. Fasten off.

Right front

Work as given for left front to **.

Shape front edge

Next row Ss over first blk and into next tr, 5ch, patt to end.
Cont to match left front, reversing shaping as shown.

Sleeves

With 4.00mm hook make 102ch and work 21 rows in patt as on Back. 100 sts, (33 blks or sps). Fasten off.

Belt

With 4.00mm hook make 15ch.
1st row 1tr in 4th ch from hook, 1tr in each of next 2ch, (2ch, miss 2ch, 1tr in next ch) twice, 1tr in each of next 3ch, (OR 1 blk, 2 sps, 1 blk).
2nd row 2 blks, 1 sp, 1 blk.
3rd row 1 blk, 2 sps, 1 blk.
4th row 1 blk, 1 sp, 2 blks.
Rep these 4 rows until belt measures about 76in/193cm, ending with a 1st or 3rd row. Fasten off.

To make up

Press according to instructions on ball band. Join shoulder seams. Sew in sleeves, placing centre of sleeves to shoulder seams. Join side and sleeve seams. With 3.50mm hook and Rs facing work a row of dc round all edges, then turn and work a second row. Press seams.

Tiffany lampshade

This elegant lampshade is worked in a fine, silky yarn and trimmed with a deep fringe

Size

Diameter at widest part 10½in/27cm
Height 7in/18cm

You will need

4 × 20g balls of fine rayon yarn
2.00mm crochet hook
Tiffany lampshade frame, size as above, with 8 sections
1 metre of fringing
Length of round elastic
The yarn quantities are based on average requirements and are therefore approximate

Tension

30 sts and 12 rows to 4in/10cm over patt worked on 2.00mm hook

To make

With 2.00mm hook make 216ch and join into a ring with a ss.

1st round 3ch as first tr, 1tr in each ch to end, ss to 3rd of first 3ch. 216tr, (72 blks).

2nd round 3ch as first tr, *1tr in each of next 3tr, (2ch miss 2tr, 1tr in next tr) 8 times, rep from * 6 times more, 1tr in each of next 3tr, (2ch, miss 2tr, 1tr in next tr) 7 times, 2ch, ss to 3rd of first 3ch, (OR (1 blk, 8 sps) 8 times).

3rd round 3ch, *1tr in each of next 3tr, (2ch, 1tr in next tr) 8 times, rep from * to end, ending as 2nd round, (OR as 2nd round).

4th round 3ch, *3tr, (2ch, 1tr in next tr) 3 times, (2tr in sp, 1tr in next tr) twice, (2ch, 1tr in next tr) 3 times, rep from * to end, but ending as 2nd round, (OR (1 blk, 3 sps, 2 blks, 3 sps) 8 times). Note that the next 12 rounds all end as 2nd round.

5th round (1 blk, 2 sps, 1 blk, 3ch, miss 2tr, 1dc in next tr, 3ch, miss 2tr, 1tr in next tr—*called 1 lacet*—1 blk, 2 sps) 8 times.

6th round (1 blk, 2 sps, 1 blk, 5ch, 1tr in next tr—*called 1 bar*—1 blk, 2 sps) 8 times.

7th round (1blk, 1 sp, 1 blk, 3ch, miss 2tr, 1dc in next tr, 3ch, miss 2ch, 1tr in next ch, 3ch, 1dc in next tr, 3ch, miss 2tr, 1tr in next tr—2 lacets—1 blk, 1 sp) 8 times.

8th round (1blk, 1 sp, 1 blk, 2 bars, 1 blk, 1 sp) 8 times.

9th round (2 blks, 3 lacets, 1blk) 8 times.

10th round (2 blks, 3 bars, 1 blk) 8 times.

11th round (1 blk, 1 sp, 1 blk, 2 lacets, 1 blk, 1 sp) 8 times.

12th round As 8th round.

13th round (1 blk, 2 sps, 1 blk, 1 lacet, 1 blk, 2 sps) 8 times.

14th round As 6th round.

15th round (1 blk, 3 sps, 5tr under bar, 1tr in next tr, 3 sps) 8 times, (OR As 4th round).

16th round As 3rd round.

17th round 3ch, *2tr, keeping last loop of each tr on work, work 1tr in each of next 2tr, yrh and draw through all 3 loops on hook—*called 2tr tog*—5 sps, 2ch, work 2tr tog, rep from * 6 times more, 2tr, 2tr tog, 6 sps, as to top of first 3ch—168 sts.

18th & 19th rounds (1 blk, 6 sps) 8 times.

20th round 3ch, *2tr, 2tr tog, 3 sps, 2ch, 2tr tog, rep from * to end, ending as 17th round—120 sts.

21st & 22nd rounds (1 blk, 4 sps) 8 times.

23rd round 3ch, *2tr, 2tr tog, 1sp, 2ch, 2tr tog, rep from * to end, ending as 17th round—72 sts.

24th & 25th rounds (1 blk, 2 sps) 8 times.

26th round 3ch, 1tr in each tr to end, ss to 3rd of first 3ch—40 sts.

Fasten off, leaving an end of yarn about 8in/20cm long.

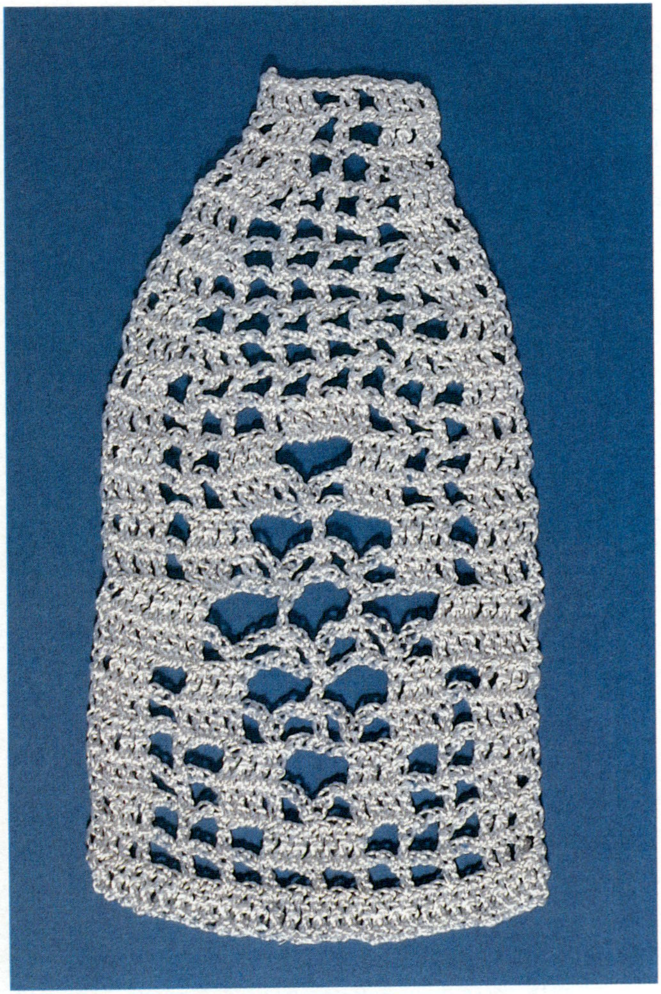

Above: ***detail showing one panel of the lampshade.***

chart for lampshade

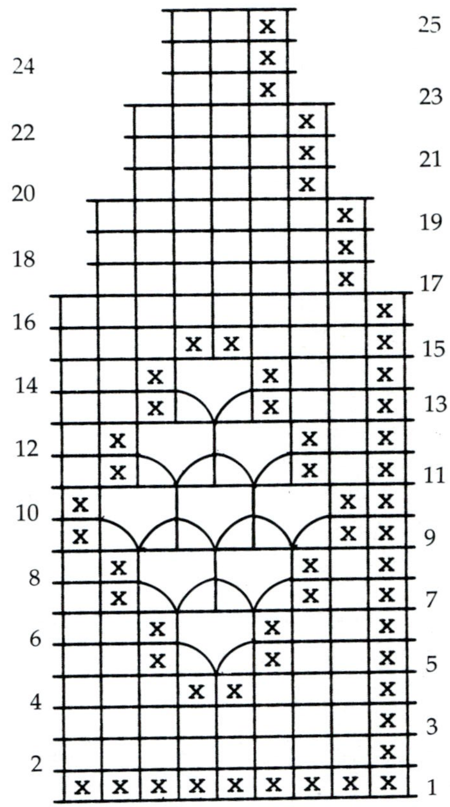

rep 9 blks or sps

To complete

Run thread through last round, draw up to size of top ring of frame and fasten securely. Run a length of round elastic through starting chain. Place shade over frame, matching the vertical lines of blks to each upright bar of frame. Draw up elastic to fit and tie securely. Stitch fringe round lower edge.

Opposite: ***this panelled lampshade is worked in the round, so the right side is always facing you. To create a soft effect, line the shade with toning or contrasting silk.***

Apricot cushion cover

A central butterfly motif highlights this cushion, and it is also worked in pure Cotton.

Size

To fit a cushion 18in/46cm square

You will need

4 × 50g balls of No 3 Cotton
4.00mm crochet hook
16in/40cm zip fastener
Cushion pad 18in/46cm square
The yarn quantities are based on average requirements and are therefore approximate

Tension

21 sts and 8 rows to 4in/10cm over patt worked on 4.00mm hook

Back and front (alike)

With 4.00mm hook make 99ch.
1st row 1tr in 4th ch from hook, 1tr in each ch to end. 97 sts, (32 blks).
2nd row 3ch as first tr, 1tr in each of next 3tr, *2ch, miss 2tr, 1tr in next tr, rep from * to last 3 sts, 1tr in each of next 2tr, 1tr in turning ch, (OR 1 blk, 30 sps, 1 blk).
3rd row 3ch, 1tr in each of next 3tr, 2ch, 1tr in next tr,

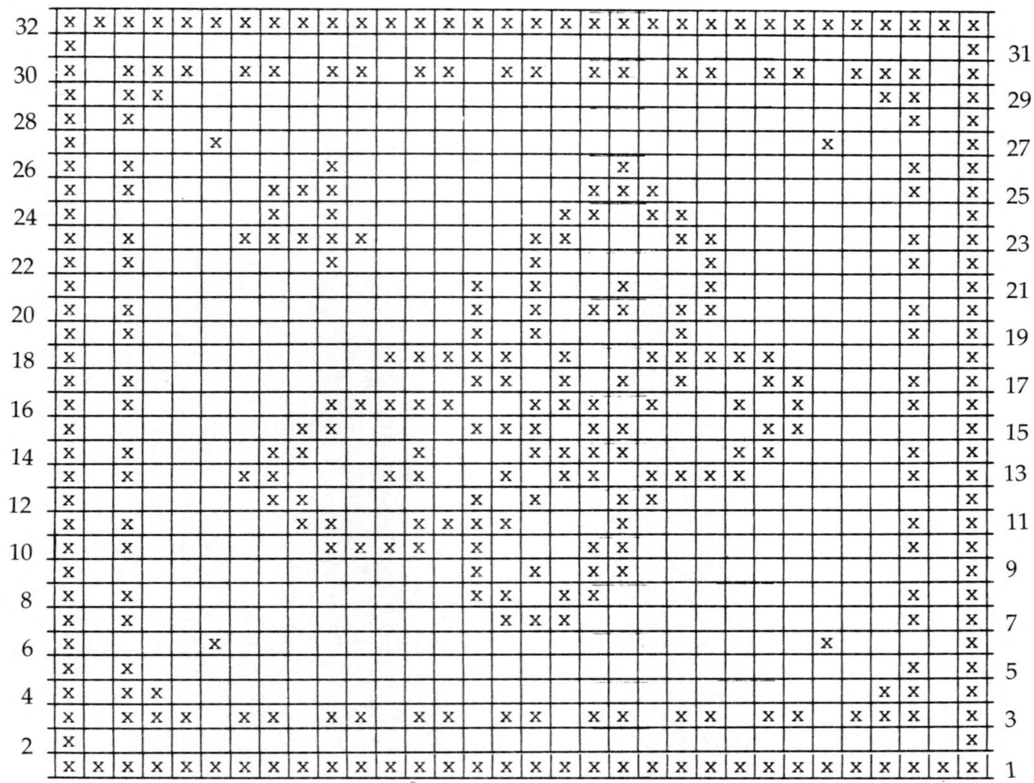

chart for apricot cushion

(1tr in sp, 1tr in next tr) 3 times, *2ch, 1tr in next tr, (2tr in sp, 1tr in next tr) twice, rep from * 7 times more, 2tr in sp, 1tr in next tr, 2ch, 1tr in each of next 3tr, 1tr in turning ch, (OR 1 blk, 1 sp, 3 blks, (1 sp, 2 blks) 8 times, 1 blk, 1 sp, 1 blk).
4th row 1 blk, 1 sp, 2 blks, 24 sps, 2 blks, 1 sp, 1 blk.
Cont in patt from chart until the 32 rows have been completed. Fasten off.

To make up
Press work according to instructions on ball band. Join 3 sides. Insert zip into 4th side, joining seam at each end as necessary.

Cushion cover

This cushion features a neat geometric motif and is worked in a pure cotton yarn.

Size
To fit a cushion 18in/46cm square

You will need
4 × 50g balls of No 3 Cotton
4.00mm crochet hook
16in/40cm zip fastener
Cushion pad 18in/46cm square
The yarn quantities are based on average requirements and are therefore approximate

Tension
21 sts and 8 rows to 4in/10cm over patt worked on 4.00mm hook

Back and front (alike)
With 4.00mm hook make 102ch.
1st row 1tr in 4th ch from hook, 1tr in each ch to end. 100 sts, (33 blks).
2nd row 3ch as first tr, 1tr in each of next 3tr, *(2ch, miss 2tr, 1tr in next tr) 15 times, 1tr in each of next 3tr, rep from * once more, working last tr in turning ch. This row reads as 1 blk, (15 sps, 1 blk) twice.
3rd row 3ch, 1tr in each of next 3tr, *2ch, 1tr in next tr, 2tr in sp, 1tr in next tr, (2ch, 1tr in next tr) 11 times, 2tr in sp, 1tr in next tr, 2ch, 1tr in each of next 4tr, rep

chart for blue cushion

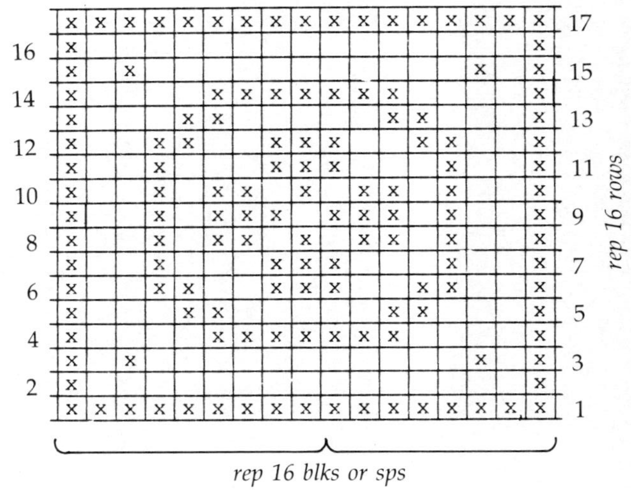

from * once more, working last tr in turning ch, (OR 1 blk, (1 sp, 1 blk, 11 sps, 1 blk, 1 sp, 1 blk) twice).
4th row 1 blk, (4 sps, 7 blks, 4 sps, 1 blk) twice.
Cont in patt from chart until the 17 rows have been completed, then work the 2nd to 17th rows again. Fasten off.

To make up
Press work according to instructions on ball band. Join 3 sides. Insert zip into 4th side, joining seam at each end as necessary.

Overleaf: ***two of a kind! One cushion cover has been worked on blue over an apricot cushion pad; the other in apricot over a blue pad.***

Mohair jersey in checked pattern

This cropped jersey has a knitted rib yoke, welt and cuffs. The filet crocheted checked pattern is simple to work.

Sizes

To fit 32[36]in/81[92]cm bust
Actual measurement 39½[44¾]in/100[114]cm
Length 20in/51cm
Sleeve seam 18in/46cm
The figures in [] refer to the 36in/92cm size only

You will need

6[7] × 50g balls of Mohair (Double Knitting weight)
4.00mm crochet hook
One pair each of 3mm and 3½mm knitting needles
The yarn quantities are based on average requirements and are therefore approximate

Tension

17 sts and 8 rows to 4in/10cm over patt worked on 4.00mm hook

Back and front (alike)

With 4.00mm hook make 87[99]ch.
1st row 1tr in 4th ch from hook, 1tr in each of next 2ch, *(2ch, miss 2ch, 1tr in next ch) twice, 1tr in each of next 6ch, rep from * to last 9ch, (2ch, miss 2ch, 1tr in next ch) twice, 1tr in each of last 3ch. This row reads as 1 blk, (2 sps, 2 blks) to last 9 sts, 2 sps, 1 blk.
2nd row 3ch as first tr, 1tr in each of next 3tr, *(2ch, 1tr in next tr) twice, 1tr in each of next 6tr, rep from * to last 10 sts, (2ch, 1tr in next tr) twice, 1tr in each of next 2tr, 1tr in turning ch. This row reads the same as 1st row.
3rd row As 2nd row.
4th row 5ch as first tr and 2ch, miss next 2tr, 1tr in next tr, *(2tr in sp, 1tr in next tr) twice, (2ch, miss 2tr, 1tr in next tr) twice, rep from * to last 9 sts, (2tr in sp, 1tr in next tr) twice, 2ch, miss 2tr, 1tr in turning ch, (OR 1 sp, (2 blks, 2 sps) to last 9 sts, 2 blks, 1sp).
Cont in patt from chart until 33 rows in all have been worked. Fasten off.

chart for mohair jersey

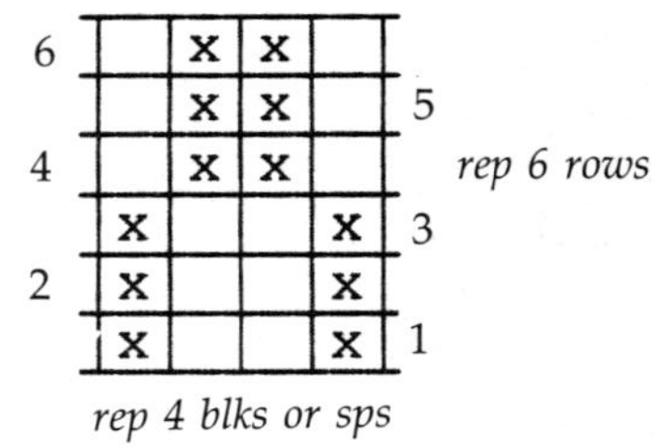

Top border

With 3½mm needles and Rs facing pick up and K106 [114] sts along top edge.
1st row K2, (P2, K2) to end.
2nd row P2, (K2, P2) to end.
Rep these 2 rows for 2in/5cm. Cast off in rib.

Welt

With 3mm needles and Rs facing pick up and K86 [98] sts along lower edge and work as for top border.

Sleeves

With 4.00mm hook make 75[87]ch and work 33 rows in pattern as on back. Fasten off.

Cuffs

With 3mm needles and Rs facing pick up and K50[54] sts along lower edge of sleeve and work as for top border.

To make up

Press work lightly according to instructions on ball band. Join shoulder seams, leaving about 10in/25cm open in centre. Sew in sleeves, placing centre of sleeves to shoulder seams. Join sides and sleeve seams. Press seams.

Above: ***soft mohair has been used for this unshaped jersey. If you don't want to knit the edges, work in double crochet or trebles instead.***

Shawl

Worked in a bright colour this makes a delightful wrap for a summer evening but use white or a pastel colour for a baby's shawl.

Size

Width across top edge, 60in/152cm
If additional width is required, work 1 more complete patt and allow 2 extra balls of yarn

You will need

10 × 50g balls of Aran weight yarn, 80% acrylic/20% wool
4.50mm crochet hook
The yarn quantity is based on average requirements and is therefore approximate

Tension

22 sts and 8 rows to 4in/10cm over filet net background worked on 4.50mm hook

Shawl centre

With 4.50 hook make 8ch.
1st row Work 1tr into 8th ch from hook to form first sp. (Note that each row is counted in sps whether blks are worked or not.)
2nd row Make 7ch and work 1tr into first st of previous row—called inc 1 sp—, 2ch, 1tr into 3rd of first 7ch, 2ch then 1 quadruple tr (yrh 4 times), into base of last tr worked—called inc 1 sp. 3 sps.
3rd row Inc 1 sp, (2ch, 1tr into next tr) twice, 2ch then 1tr into 3rd of first 7ch—called work last sp. 4 sps.
4th row Inc 1 sp, (2ch, 1tr into next tr) 3 times, work last sp. 5 sps.
5th row Inc 1 sp, (2ch, 1tr into next tr) 4 times, work last sp, inc 1 sp. 7 sps.
6th row Inc 1 sp, (2 ch, 1tr into next tr) 6 times, work last sp. 8 sps.
7th row Inc 1 sp, (2ch, 1tr into next tr) 7 times, work last sp. 9 sps.
8th row Inc 1 sp, (4 sps, 1 blk, 4 sps working last tr into 3rd of first 7ch) for motif, inc 1 sp. 11 sps.
9th row Inc 1 sp, 1 sp, (3 sps, 3 blks, 3 sps) for motif, work last sp. 12 sps.
10th row Inc 1 sp, 1 sp, (3 sps, 3 blks, 3 sps) for motif, 1 sp, work last sp. 13 sps.
11th row Inc 1 sp, 2 sps, (1 sp, 2 blks, 1 sl, 1 blk, 1 sp, 2 blks, 1 sp) for motif, 1 sp, work last sp, inc 1 sp. 15 sps.
12th row Inc 1 sp, 3 sps, (4 blks, 1 sp, 4 blks) for motif, 2 sps, work last sp. 16 sps.
13th row Inc 1 sp, 3 sps, (1 sp, 2 blks, 1 sp, 1 blk, 1 sp, 2 blks, 1 sp) for motif, 3 sps, work last sp. 17 sps.
14th row Inc 1 sp, 4 sps, (3 sps, 3 blks, 3 sps) for motif, 3 sps, work last sp, inc 1 sp. 19 sps.
15th row Inc 1 sp, 5 sps, (3 sps, 3 blks, 3 sps) for motif, 4 sps, work last sp. 20 sps.
16th row Inc 1 sp, 5 sps, (4 sps, 1 blk, 4 sps) for motif, 5 sps, work last sp. 21 sps.
17th row Inc 1 sp, work sps all across row, inc 1 sp. 23 sps.
18th row Inc 1 sp, work sps all across row. 24 sps.
19th row Inc 1 sp, work sps all across row. 25 sps.
20th row Inc 1 sp, (4 sps, 1 blk, 4 sps) for motif, 7 sps, (4 sps, 1 blk, 4 sps working last tr into 3rd of first 7ch), inc 1 sp. 27 sps.

Opposite: ***this elegant shawl is practical and warm. The fringing is simply crochet chains, so there is no problem with trying to keep cut ends all to the same length!***

21st row Inc 1 sp, 1 sp, (3 sps, 3 blks, 3 sps) for motif, 7 sps, (3 sps, 3 blks, 3 sps), 1 sp. 28 sps.
22nd row Inc 1 sp, 1 sp, (3 sps, 3 blks, 3 sps) for motif, 7 sps, (3 sps, 3 blks, 3 sps), 2 sps. 29 sps.
23rd row Inc 1 sp, 2 sps, (1 sp, 2 blks, 1 sp, 1 blk, 1 sp, 2 blks, 1 sp) for motif, 7 sps, (1 sp, 2 blks, 1 sp, 1 blk, 1 sp, 2 blks, 1 sp), 1 sp, work last sp, inc 1 sp. 31 sps.
24th row Inc 1 sp, 3 sps, (4 blks, 1 sp, 4 blks) for motif, 7 sps, (4 blks, 1 sp, 4 blks), 2 sps, work last sp. 32 sps.
25th row Inc 1 sp, 3 sps, (1 sp, 2 blks, 1 sp, 1 blk, 1 sp) for motif, 7 sps, (1 sp, 2 blks, 1 sp, 2 blks, 1 sp), 3 sps, work last sp, 22 sps.
26th row Inc 1 sp, 4 sps, (3 sps, 3 blks, 3 sps) for motif, 7 sps, (3 sps, 3 blks, 3 sps), 3 sps, work last sp, inc 1 sp. 35 sps.
27th row Inc 1 sp, 5 sps, (3 sps, 3 blks, 3 sps) for motif, 7 sps, (3 sps, 3 blks, 3 sps), 4 sps, work last sp. 36 sps.
28th row Inc 1 sp, 5 sps, (4 sps, 1 blk, 4 sps) for motif, 7 sps, (4 sps, 1 blk, 4 sps), 5 sps, work last sp. 37 sps.
29th row As 17th.
30th row As 18th.
31st row As 19th. 41 sps.
Cont in this way, rep 20th to 31st rows inclusive and inc 4 sps over every 3 rows, with 7 sps between each motif on each rep, until there are 105 sps, noting that next row will read as foll:-
32nd row Inc 1 sp, *(4 sps, 1 blk, 4 sps) for motif, 7 sps, *, rep from * to * once, (4 sps, 1 blk, 4 sps), inc 1 sp.
Do not break off yarn at end of last row.

chart for shawl

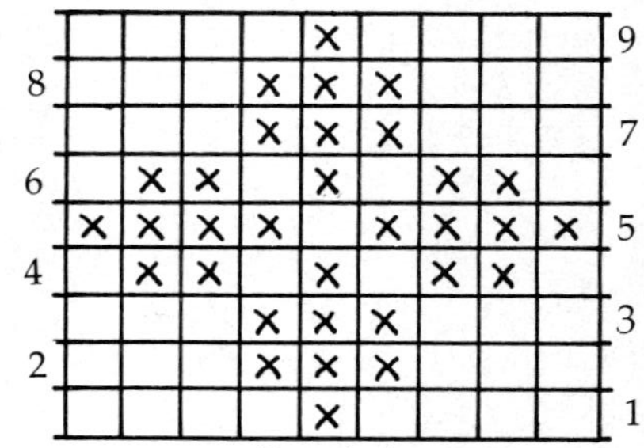

motif worked over
9 sps and 9 rows

Fringing

With 4.50mm hook, into each row end along side edge *(work 1dc, 4ch, 1dc)*, into commencing sp (work 1dc, 40ch) 4 times, 1dc), rep from * to * along other side edge.
Do not break off yarn.

Top edge

With 4.50mm hook into first sp along top edge *work (1dc, 1htr, 1tr, 1htr, 1dc), 1ch, 1dc into next ch sp, 1ch, rep from * to last sp, work (1dc, 1htr, 1tr, 1htr, 1dc) into last sp.
Fasten off.

To complete

Do not press. Darn in all ends.

Cafe curtain

A jaunty windmill motif is featured on this cotton cafe curtain, making it ideal for a kitchen window.

Size

Width 41in/104cm
Depth 18in/46cm to top of tabs

You will need

5 × 50g balls of No 3 Cotton
4.00mm crochet hook
The yarn quantities are based on average requirements and are therefore approximate

Tension

21 sts and 9 rows to 4in/10cm over patt worked on 4.00mm hook

To make

With 4.00mm hook make 222ch.
1st row 1tr in 4th ch from hook, 1tr in each ch to end. 220tr, (73 blks).
2nd row 3ch as first tr, 1tr in each of next 3tr, *2ch, miss 2tr, 1tr in next tr, rep from * to last 3 sts, 1tr in each of next 2tr, 1tr in turning ch. This row reads as 1 blk, 71 sps, 1 blk.
3rd row 3ch, 1tr in each of next 3tr, *2ch, 1tr in next tr, rep from * to last 3 sts, 1tr in each of next 2tr, 1tr in turning ch. This row reads as 1st row.
4th row As 3rd row.
5th row 3ch, 1tr in each of next 3tr, (2ch, 1tr in next tr) 10 times, (2tr in sp, 1tr in next tr) 20 times, (2ch, 1tr in next tr) 11 times, (2tr in sp, 1tr in next tr) 20 times, (2ch, 1tr in next tr) 10 times, 1tr in each of next 2tr, 1tr in turning ch, (OR 1 blk, 10 sps, 20 blks, 11 sps, 20 blks, 10 sps, 1 blk).
6th row 1 blk, 11 sps, 18 blks, 13 sps, 18 blks, 11 sps, 1 blk.
Cont in patt from chart until the 25 rows have been completed, then rep 3rd row 9 times.

Make tabs

Next row 1 blk, 2 sps, turn and work 5 more rows on these sts. Fasten off. *Miss 4 sps, rejoin yarn to next tr, 5ch, 1tr in next tr, (2ch, 1tr in next tr) twice, turn and work 5 more rows on these 3 sps. Fasten off. Rep from * 6 times more. Miss next 4 sps, rejoin yarn to next tr, 5ch, 1tr in next tr, 2ch, 1tr in next tr, 1tr in each of next 2tr, 1tr in turning ch. Work 5 more rows on these sts. Fasten off.

To complete

Press work according to instructions on ball band. Fold tabs in half to wrong side and stitch in place. Press seams.

See front cover and page 10 for illustrations and overleaf for chart.

chart for cafe curtain

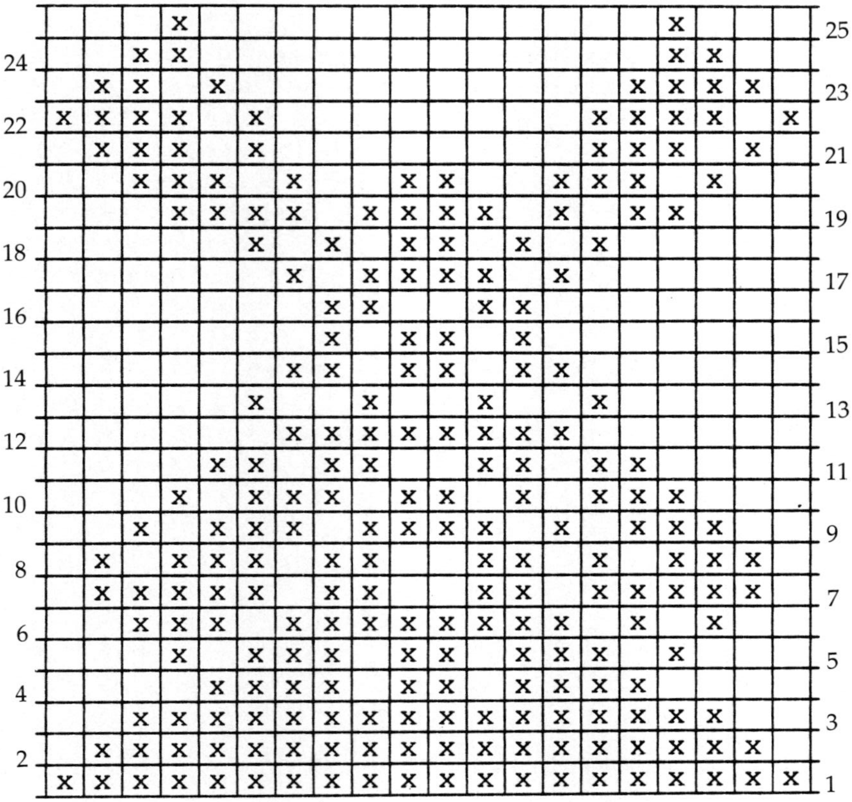

Baby's angel top

Fit for an angel! This dainty top has an angel motif worked on the front skirt.

Size

To fit 18in/46cm chest
Length 12in/30cm
Sleeve seam 7in/18cm

You will need

2 × 50g balls of Baby 4ply
3.00mm crochet hook
3 buttons
The yarn quantities are based on average requirements and are therefore approximate

Tension

24 sts and 10 rows to 4in/10cm over pattern worked on 3.00mm hook

Front

With 3.00mm hook make 101ch.
1st row 1tr in 8th ch from hook, *2ch, miss 2ch, 1tr in next ch, rep from * to end. 97 sts, (32 sps).
2nd row 5ch as first tr and 2ch, 1tr in next tr, *2ch, 1tr in next tr, rep from * to end, working last tr in 3rd of first 5ch.
3rd row 5ch, 1tr in next tr, (2ch, 1tr in next tr) 11 times, 2tr in sp, 1tr in next tr, (2ch, 1tr in next tr) to end, working last tr in 3rd of first 5ch, (OR 22 sps, 1 blk, 9 sps).
4th row 9 sps, 2 blks, 21 sps.
Cont in patt from chart until the 14 rows have been completed, **, then work 4 rows in sps. Fasten off.

Shape armholes

With Rs facing miss first 4 sps, rejoin yarn to next tr, 3ch as first tr, 1tr in sp, 1tr in next tr, *(1tr in next tr, 1tr in sp) twice, 1tr in next tr, rep from * 6 times more,

chart for angel top

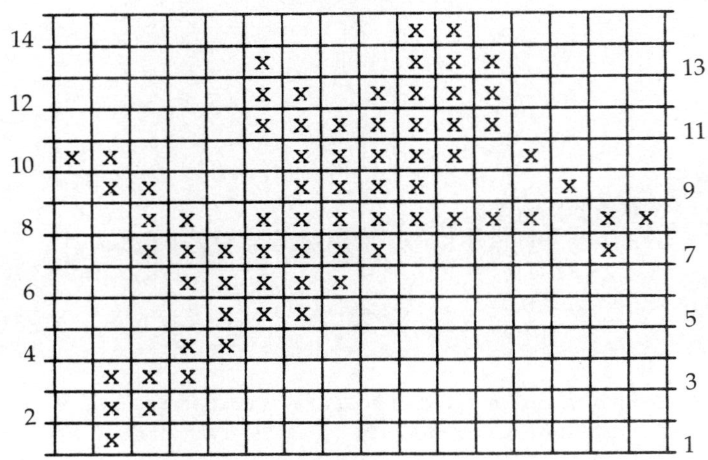

Above: ***this little top buttons at the back yoke and can be worn over a dress, rompers or dungarees. The neck, cuffs and lower edge are finished with crab stitch, which is simply double crochet worked backwards along the row from left to right.***

1tr in next tr, 1tr in sp, 1tr in next tr, turn, leaving 4 sps unworked. 41 sts.
Next row 3ch, 1tr in each tr to end.
Rep the last row 5 times more.

Shape neck

Next row 3ch, 12tr, turn and cont on these 13 sts.
Dec one st at neck edge on next 3 rows. 10 sts. Fasten off.
Return to where work was left, miss centre 15 sts, rejoin yarn to next tr, 3ch, work to end. Cont to match first side.

Back

Work as given for Front as far as **.
Next row Work 16 sps, turn and work 3 more rows in sps on these sts. Fasten off.

Shape armhole

Next row With Rs facing miss first 4 sps, rejoin yarn to next tr, 3ch, 1tr in sp, 1tr in next tr, *(1tr in next tr, 1tr in sp) twice, 1tr in next tr, rep from * twice more, 1tr in next tr, 1tr in sp, 1tr in next tr, turn. 21 sts.
Work 9 rows in tr.

Shape neck

Next row 3ch, 9tr, turn and fasten off.
Return to where work was left, rejoin yarn to same tr as last st of first side, 3ch, 1tr in sp, 1tr in next tr, rep from * on same row on first side, leaving 4 sps unworked. 21 sts.
Cont to match first side, reversing shaping.

Sleeves

With 3.00mm hook make 53ch and work 1st row as on back. 49 sts, (16 sps).
Cont in sps throughout until sleeve measures 6¼in/16cm. Place a marker at each end of last row, then work a further 5 rows. Fasten off.
Cuff With Rs facing rejoin yarn to starting ch, 1ch as first dc, (1dc in next tr, 1dc in sp, 1dc in next tr) to end. 25 sts.
Work 4 more rows in dc, then 1 row crab st. Fasten off.

To make up

Press work according to instructions on ball band.
Join shoulder seams. Sew in sleeves, sewing the last 5 rows of sleeve seams to the 4 sps at armholes. Join side and sleeve seams.
With Rs facing, work 1 row of dc and 1 row crab st round neck and lower edge. Work 2 rows of dc round back opening, making 3 button loops on right back edge. Sew 3 buttons to left back to correspond.
Press seams.

More about filet crochet

This particular crochet technique produces an openwork, lacy fabric, and care needs to be taken with the final stages of making up to avoid hard and clumsy seams.

Similarly, rough handling during laundering will snag the fabric and distort the crispness of the background net and definition of the motifs.

Choosing yarns

It is always safest to use the yarn specified in the pattern, see page 48 for details. The design, texture, colours, tension and the amount needed will all have been carefully calculated on that product. It *is* possible to use a substitute, if you cannot obtain the brand given in the instructions, but you must experiment with tension samples until you can achieve the correct tension. Also, don't expect the texture of the design to look the same as that shown in the illustration and remember that the quantities given will vary.

Blocking

This is the term given to the stage of pinning out each section to the correct size and shape, before pressing. Filet crochet fabrics benefit if they are pinned out in this way and left under a damp cloth for a few hours; this is essential if the yarn you have used cannot be pressed.

Pressing

This is not always essential or even advisable. Always keep a ball band from the yarn you are using, as this will tell you if the yarn can be pressed and the correct iron temperature setting.

Many of the yarns available today are blends of man-made fibres, some of which should *never* be pressed. If you are in any doubt, *do not press*.

Seams

These should be worked on the wrong side of the fabric joining the edges of two pieces together by taking half-a-stitch from each edge, and working an oversewn seam.

Assemble the pieces in the order given in the instructions, pinning them together to ensure that patterns match exactly. Use a blunt-ended sewing needle and the original yarn; if this is too thick or fluffy, use a finer yarn in the same colour.

Aftercare

Time and skill will have gone into making the designs featured in this book and it is important to realise that as much care must be taken in laundering these items.

Because of the lacy structure of filet crochet, it is not advisable to machine-wash the fabric. The following suggestions will help keep your garments in pristine condition:

1) Use a detergent or soap specially recommended for delicate garments. This will dissolve easily and will not contain harmful bleach, more suitable for household linens.

2) Beware of adding so much soap, or detergent, that it is difficult to remove during rinsing.

3) Never soak crochet fabrics; wash them frequently and keep the washing process brief.

4) Avoid very hot water.

5) Hand-wash by gently squeezing; don't lift the garment out of the water or the weight will distort the shape.

6) Rinse very thoroughly, then gently squeeze out as much water as you can. Do *not* spin-dry.

7) To dry, pad a table with newspaper then cover this with a thick, white or colour-fast towel. Place the garment on this, gently patting it into shape – make sure the background net retains its crisp outlines and that the motifs have not been pulled out of shape.

8) Leave the garment to dry away from direct heat or sunlight. If necessary, replace the wet newspaper with fresh sheets. For a final airing, a garment can be pegged from under the arms on a line but never peg from the shoulders.

Comparative hook sizes

The following list is intended as a guide only, as the sizes are not exact equivalents:

Metric sizes	*Old UK sizes*		*USA sizes*
	Wool	*Cotton*	
7.00	2	–	K/10½
–	3	–	–
6.00	4	–	J/10
5.50	5	–	I/9
5.00	6	–	H/8
4.50	7	–	G/6
4.00	8	–	F/5
3.50	9	–	E/4
3.00	10	3/0	D/3
			C/2
–	11	2/0	–
2.50	12	0	B/1
–	13	1	–
2.00	14	1½	–
–	–	2	–
1.75	15	2½	–
–	–	3	–
1.50	16	3½	–
–	–	4	–
1.25	–	4½	–
–	–	5	–
1.00	–	5½	–
–	–	6	–
0.75	–	6½	–
0.50	–	7	–
–	–	7½	–

Comparative terminology

The basic stitches in crochet are worked one step behind in America, as follows:

British	*American*
chain (ch)	chain (ch)
slip stitch (ss)	slip stitch (ss)
double crochet (dc)	single crochet (sc)
half treble (htr)	half double crochet (hdc)
treble	double crochet (dc)
double treble	treble (tr)
triple treble	double treble (dtr)

First published in Great Britain 1989
Search Press Ltd.,
Wellwood, North Farm Road,
Tunbridge Wells, Kent TN2 3DR.

Text, pram cover and shawl designs by Pam Dawson
Other designs and filet charts by Jean Litchfield
Technical drawings by Jan Messent
Photographs by Search Press Studios

ISBN 0 85532 620 4

List of yarns featured in this book

Angel top, *Patons Fairytale 4 ply*
Beach wrap, *Wendy Seta Silken Style*
Mohair jersey, *Pingouin Mohair 50*
Cafe curtain, *Patons Cotton Perlé*
Cushions, *Twilleys Stalite Perléspun No. 3*
Pram cover, *Wendy Peter Pan Darling DK*
Shawl, *Phildar Pegase 206*
Tiffany lampshade, *Twilleys Lystwist, rayon*

Typeset by Scribe Design, 123 Watling Street, Gillingham, Kent
Made and printed in Spain by A. G. Elkar, S. Coop. 48012-Bilbao.